WORLD WAR II
TURNING POINTS

BY JOHN HAMILTON

VISIT US AT
WWW.ABDOPUBLISHING.COM

Published by ABDO Publishing Company, 8000 West 78th Street, Suite 310, Edina, MN 55439. Copyright ©2012 by Abdo Consulting Group, Inc. International copyrights reserved in all countries. No part of this book may be reproduced in any form without written permission from the publisher. ABDO & Daughters™ is a trademark and logo of ABDO Publishing Company.

Printed in the United States of America, North Mankato, Minnesota.
052011
092011

♻ PRINTED ON RECYCLED PAPER

Editor: Sue Hamilton
Graphic Design: John Hamilton
Cover Design: Neil Klinepier
Cover Photo: National Archives and Records Administration (NARA)
Interior Photos and Illustrations: Getty Images, p. 1, 6-7, 8, 9, 10, 11, 12-13, 13 (*Mikuma*), 14-15, 16, 18, 19, 20-21, 21, 22-23, 27, 29; John Hamilton, p. 4, 7, 12, 15, 16, 20, 23, 25, 27; NARA, p. 3, 5, 17, 24-25, 26, 28, 31; U.S. Navy, p. 13 (Dauntless bombers).

ABDO Booklinks

To learn more about World War II, visit ABDO Publishing Company online. Web sites about World War II are featured on our Book Links pages. These links are routinely monitored and updated to provide the most current information available. Web site: www.abdopublishing.com

Library of Congress Cataloging-in-Publication Data

Hamilton, John, 1959-
 World War II. Turning points / John Hamilton.
    p. cm. -- (World War II)
 Includes index.
 ISBN 978-1-61783-062-4
 1. World War, 1939-1945--Campaigns--Juvenile literature. I. Title. II. Title: Turning points.
 D743.7.H36 2012
 940.54'2--dc22
                2011015969

CONTENTS

U.S. Marines in the Solomon Islands

TURNING POINTS OF
WWII

By mid-1942, after nearly three years of bloody, bitter warfare, the Axis alliance of Germany, Japan, and Italy seemed unstoppable. German *blitzkrieg* attacks had swallowed up most of Europe. In the Pacific, the Japanese empire continued to expand, conquering island after island and spreading to mainland China and other Asian nations.

On December 7, 1941, Japan attacked the United States naval base at Pearl Harbor, Hawaii. The United States finally declared war and threw its manpower and industrial might into the struggle.

In the following three years, the Allies, including the United States, Great Britain, and the Soviet Union, began turning the tide of the war with battlefield successes.

By mid-1942, Nazi Germany and its allies had conquered much of Europe and North Africa.

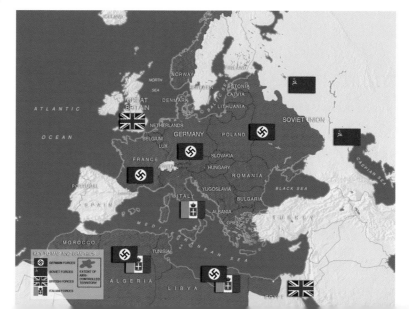

A German trooper's face shows the misery of winter fighting in the Soviet Union. At the Battle of Stalingrad, during the winter of 1942–1943, at least half a million Axis troops were killed or wounded, either by fighting, cold, or hunger. Another 91,000 were captured. After this major defeat, the Germans were pushed slowly west out of the Soviet Union.

THE DESERT WAR: NORTH AFRICA

O n June 10, 1940, Italian dictator Benito Mussolini threw his country's support behind Nazi Germany and declared war on France and Great Britain. One of his first acts was to use Italy's colony of Libya from which to launch attacks against Egypt. The prize—the Suez Canal, the lifeline through which Great Britain was able to send and receive supplies from Asia.

The "Desert Rats" of the British Seventh Armoured Division, together with Australian and other Commonwealth troops, mounted a furious counterattack. The Allies decimated the inferior Italian forces. In response, Germany's Adolf Hitler sent fresh troops to North Africa, including a newly created desert-fighting force, the *Afrika Korps*, led by famed tank commander Erwin Rommel.

British troops rolling across the Libyan desert in Carden-Loyd tracked vehicles.

KEY TO MAP AND GRAPHICS

- German Forces
- American Forces
- British Forces
- Italian Forces

EXTENT OF AXIS-CONTROLLED TERRITORY

In the final months of the North Africa campaign, a combined Allied effort by American, British, and other Commonwealth nations pushed German and Italian forces into Tunisia. By the spring of 1943, more than 200,000 cornered Axis troops surrendered.

1940–1943

German Field Marshal Erwin Rommel

For tank commanders, the desert was an ideal place to fight. There were few obstacles, towns, or civilians to get in the way. Antitank guns and mines were a danger, but desert fighting was like a sea battle, with both sides sweeping across oceans of sand in search of an elusive enemy.

At first, the *Afrika Korps* achieved many victories over the British. Led by the crafty and daring Field Marshal Rommel— the "Desert Fox"—the Germans pushed the British back, deep into Egyptian territory.

Fighting took place along the North African coast. Supplies were always a problem, especially water for the men and gasoline for the tanks and other vehicles. The hot desert climate made fighting difficult for the troops. The constant, swirling dust was hard on machinery, especially airplanes.

In August 1942, the British Eighth Army in Egypt welcomed a new commander—General Bernard Montgomery. Although he raised the troops' morale with his spirited personality, he was a cautious general. He only committed his army to battle when he felt thoroughly prepared with overwhelming force. Some felt Montgomery was weak because he was not bold or creative. But he soon proved his critics wrong at the Battle of El Alamein.

German troops take cover as British bombs pound their defensive positions in Tunisia.

British General Bernard Montgomery watches the movement of his tank formations during the North Africa campaign.

The small village of El Alamein lies on the Egyptian coast just west of the city of Alexandria. With a force of more than 1,000 tanks and 200,000 troops, it was at El Alamein that General Montgomery forced Rommel and the *Afrika Korps* to crack.

The attack began on the night of October 23, 1942. After a thunderous artillery barrage, the British forces advanced through treacherous minefields, and then engaged the enemy.

Following several days of fierce battle, the Germans were forced to begin a long withdrawal westward, back into Libya and Tunisia. With their gasoline supply dwindling, the Germans littered the desert with dead men and the burned-out hulks of tanks.

A British Valentine tank advances during the Battle of El Alamein.

Meanwhile, American forces landed in Morocco and Algeria on November 8, 1942. The invasion was called Operation Torch. The Americans attacked the Germans from the west, adding to the pressure. Hitler sent reinforcements to North Africa, which weakened his European defenses.

The inexperienced Americans suffered a terrible defeat at Kasserine Pass in Tunisia in February 1943. But under the new leadership of U.S. Army General George S. Patton, the Americans began driving the *Afrika Korps* back to the sea, cornering them in Tunisia.

The Germans and Italians fought until the spring of 1943, but they were finally defeated. More than 200,000 Axis soldiers surrendered. The tide of war at last was beginning to change.

American General George S. Patton

11

The BATTLE OF MIDWAY

In June 1942, the Japanese navy set out to cripple the United States once and for all. Earlier losses at the Battle of the Coral Sea convinced Japanese Admiral Isoroku Yamamoto to attack the small American military base at Midway Island, northwest of Hawaii. He hoped to lure the American fleet, with its powerful aircraft carriers, into a trap and crush it, allowing Japan free reign in the Pacific.

The Americans, however, had broken the Japanese radio codes. U.S. Admiral Chester Nimitz sent American ships to intercept the Japanese battle fleet.

Between June 4 and 6, Japanese and American naval aircraft pounded each other's fleets. The American aircraft carrier *Yorktown* was crippled and later sank.

For the Japanese, the battle was a disaster. Four aircraft carriers and a cruiser were sunk, with other ships heavily damaged. Also lost were hundreds of planes and thousands of men, including experienced pilots and mechanics.

BATTLE OF MIDWAY

JAPAN

UNITED STATES

Pacific Ocean

HAWAII

The Battle of Midway was fought mainly by aircraft. Japanese and American surface ships were never in sight of each other.

Dauntless dive bomber

Japanese cruiser *Mikuma*

Dive bombers inflicted terrible damage to both fleets. Planes such as the American Dauntless (above left) and Japanese Val dove almost vertically and released their bombs. Fuel and ammunition on enemy ships often exploded when the dive bombers struck their targets. Above right, the Japanese heavy cruiser *Mikuma* was heavily damaged during the battle and sank.

JUNE 1942

The BATTLE OF GUADALCANAL

Just two months after its victory at the Battle of Midway, the United States and its allies for the first time began a major offensive push against Japan and its empire in the Pacific Ocean. The first goal was Guadalcanal, a small tropical island in the southern end of the Solomon Islands, east of New Guinea.

Japan had recently invaded Guadalcanal and begun building an airfield. The United States knew that it would threaten vital supply routes between the U.S., Australia, and New Zealand. It had to be captured at all costs.

On August 7, 1942, United States Marines landed on Guadalcanal. Assisted by U.S. Navy ships, within days the Marines overwhelmed the Japanese defenders. They renamed the airfield Henderson Field, and prepared to use it for further attacks against Japan.

The Japanese leadership was surprised by the American assault. They responded almost immediately, sending thousands of reinforcements to retake the airfield. The Americans sent in even more troops, ships, and airplanes. The coming battle promised to be long and bloody.

United States Marines storming the beaches of Guadalcanal. The Marines were experts at landing from the sea, which is called amphibious warfare. They were often the first ones to attack the many Pacific Ocean islands defended by Japanese forces. The Marines of World War II, like those of today, were well trained, very tough, and could fight and survive even in terrible conditions.

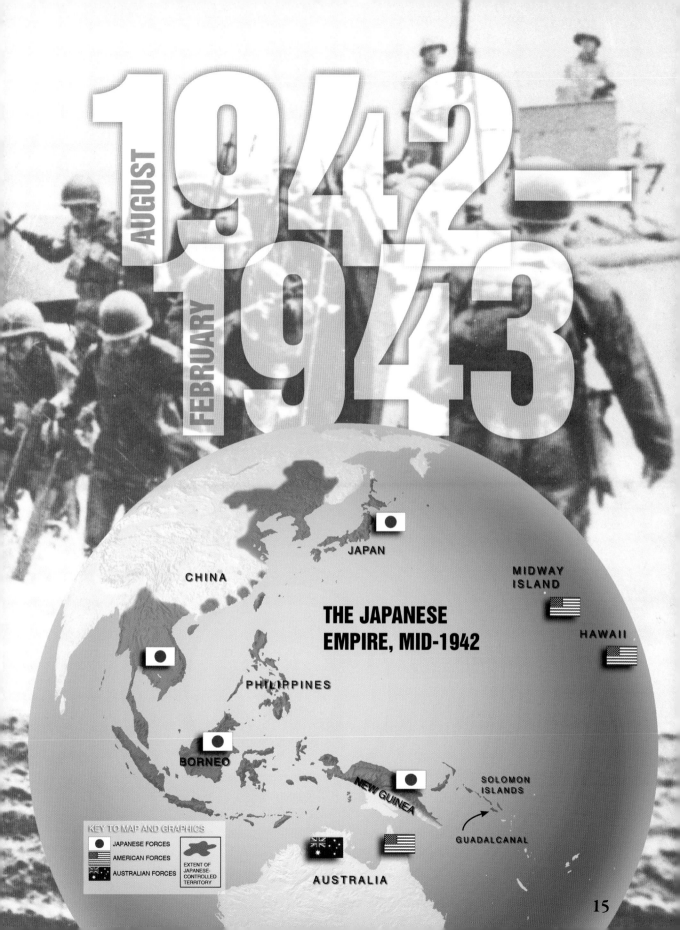

AUGUST

FEBRUARY

1942– 1943

THE JAPANESE EMPIRE, MID-1942

JAPAN

CHINA

MIDWAY ISLAND

HAWAII

PHILIPPINES

BORNEO

NEW GUINEA

SOLOMON ISLANDS

GUADALCANAL

AUSTRALIA

KEY TO MAP AND GRAPHICS

JAPANESE FORCES

AMERICAN FORCES

AUSTRALIAN FORCES

EXTENT OF JAPANESE-CONTROLLED TERRITORY

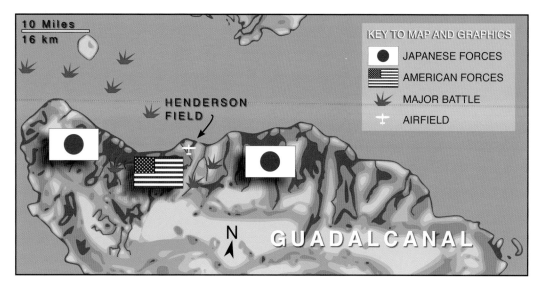

10 Miles
16 km

KEY TO MAP AND GRAPHICS
● JAPANESE FORCES
🇺🇸 AMERICAN FORCES
✲ MAJOR BATTLE
✛ AIRFIELD

HENDERSON FIELD

N

GUADALCANAL

The Battle of Guadalcanal was a test for both sides. It pitted the Allies' fighting capability against Japan's desire to hold onto its newly conquered empire.

Jungle warfare was especially harsh. Dense tropical forests, heat, constant rainfall, insects, and snakes were common hazards. Diseases such as malaria and dysentery added to the soldiers' misery. The fighting itself was often savage. Well-concealed enemies seemed to pop up out of nowhere, resulting in hand-to-hand combat to the death.

During a nighttime battle on August 8-9, 1942, the Imperial Navy sank four U.S. cruisers. The American Navy was forced to withdraw, leaving a force of U.S. Marines to defend Henderson Field. The Marines dug in with machine guns and artillery.

On August 21, the Japanese attacked in human waves. Many screamed *banzai* as they threw themselves into battle.

American Marines seek out the enemy in a jungle region of Guadalcanal.

Antiaircraft fire explodes above the American aircraft carrier *Enterprise*, left, and other ships during the Battle of Santa Cruz, October 26, 1942, part of the struggle to secure Guadalcanal. An explosion can be seen near the *Enterprise*. A Japanese dive bomber appears in the center of the photo. To the right, the battleship *South Dakota* is seen firing its antiaircraft guns.

Although terrifying, the Japanese massed assaults were ineffective. During the first wave, almost all of the 900 attacking Japanese were killed. About 40 Americans died. The Battle of Bloody Ridge on September 12 had similar results.

After regrouping, the U.S. Navy was able to engage the enemy. At night, the Japanese were supplying reinforcements of men and supplies to the island. The "Tokyo Express," as it was called, had to be stopped.

A series of five major naval battles for control of the island shut down the Japanese supply route, but at a high cost: more than 5,000 American sailors were killed. About 3,500 Japanese sailors also died. Many ships from both sides were sunk, including the American aircraft carrier *Hornet*.

By December, the Americans had a definite advantage, using land, air, and sea units in a combined arms assault against the remaining Japanese forces. U.S. Army troops also joined the battle, relieving the exhausted Marines, who had fought nonstop for many weeks.

In February 1943, the Japanese finally abandoned Guadalcanal. They evacuated most of their remaining troops, about 11,000 soldiers, under cover of darkness.

Less than 1,000 Japanese soldiers were taken prisoner on Guadalcanal. More than 20,000 were killed. The Japanese also lost 15 warships and about 850 planes. The United States suffered about 6,000 casualties, including 1,752 soldiers killed.

The American victory at Guadalcanal came at a high price. For the Japanese, the cost was even more steep. Not only did they

United States Marines lead a group of weary and starving Japanese prisoners to a beach on Guadalcanal. The prospect of being captured was deeply disgraceful to most Japanese soldiers. Many fought to the death rather than be taken prisoner.

lose men and equipment, their determination to retake the island meant that their other operations in the Pacific suffered. After the battle, they were forced to retreat and regroup. From this point on, they would be on the defensive, against an Allied force that grew stronger with each passing month.

Opposite page: Exhausted United States Marines sprawl on a tropical beach on Guadalcanal. They are awaiting a landing craft, which will take them off the island following months of fighting the Japanese.

The BATTLE OF STALINGRAD

During much of 1942, the German army fought its way east across the vast Soviet Union. But by late summer, at the city of Stalingrad in southwestern Russia, the Nazi push came to a halt.

Stalingrad (today's Volgograd) was a large industrial city on the Volga River. During the German invasion, most of the city's residents were evacuated. After months of pounding from German aircraft, tanks, and artillery, most of the city was reduced to rubble.

Fighting inside Stalingrad was desperate and brutal. Eventually, the Soviet Union's Red Army, led by General Vasily Chuikov, encircled and trapped thousands of Germans inside the city, cutting them off from food and supplies.

Casualties, winter weather, and a lack of supplies finally forced the German commander, Field Marshal Friedrich Paulus, to surrender what remained of his army, about 91,000 men.

The Germans never recovered from the defeat at Stalingrad. The Soviets slowly began pushing them back to the west.

Soviet General Vasily Chuikov said of the defense of Stalingrad: "We will defend the city or die in the attempt." The Soviets won the battle, but at a terrible cost: combined Soviet and German casualties were about two million killed or wounded, including soldiers and civilians.

AUGUST 1942-FEBRUARY 1943

Below left: Two German soldiers pinned down in house-to-house fighting in Stalingrad. *Below right:* A German Panzer VI Tiger tank at the Battle of Kursk. Shortly after the German defeat at Stalingrad, both sides fought with thousands of tanks and aircraft in the summer of 1943 in southwestern Russia. The Red Army won the battle, ending any real German hope of defeating the Soviet Union.

The INVASION OF SICILY

In July 1943, American and British forces launched an assault on the southern coast of the Italian island of Sicily.

Control of Sicily would make Allied shipping lanes through the Mediterranean Sea safer. The battle would also cause Germany to divert soldiers and supplies away from the rest of Europe.

The invasion force was led by American General George Patton and British General Bernard Montgomery. Just six weeks after the Allies landed, the Axis army had no choice but to evacuate to the Italian mainland.

Italy's humiliated Benito Mussolini soon lost power. The new government switched sides, but the Germans took over, preventing an easy Allied invasion of the mainland. Months of bloody fighting were ahead for the Allies, but the Axis powers were beginning to crumble.

American troops patrol a war-ravaged street in Messina, on the island of Sicily. The Americans and British were welcomed by most Italians as liberators.

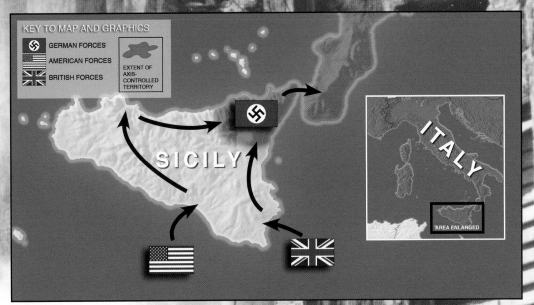

KEY TO MAP AND GRAPHICS

GERMAN FORCES

AMERICAN FORCES

BRITISH FORCES

EXTENT OF AXIS-CONTROLLED TERRITORY

SICILY

ITALY

AREA ENLARGED

The Allied invasion of Sicily was code named Operation Husky. The invasion began on July 10, 1943, with a combined amphibious landing of troops, naval bombardment, and air assault. The Allies pushed northward, driving Axis troops to the northeast of Sicily, and finally off the island.

JULY 1943–AUGUST 1943

The NORMANDY INVASION: D-DAY

By the spring of 1944, much progress had been made against the Axis powers. The Japanese empire shrank with each passing week. The Germans were suffering terrible losses against the Red Army of the Soviet Union. Even so, Allied leaders knew that to defeat Adolf Hitler and Nazi Germany, they had to invade and liberate Europe, starting in France.

United States President Franklin D. Roosevelt and British Prime Minister Winston Churchill, together with the other Allied countries, drew up plans to invade northern France from the south of England. American General Dwight D. Eisenhower was named Supreme Allied Commander of what would be known as Operation Overlord. It would be the largest invasion in history.

On D-Day, many Allied troops made their final assault in Higgins boats. In this photo, the boat's ramp has dropped down, allowing the infantry to wade ashore at Omaha Beach—directly into heavy enemy fire.

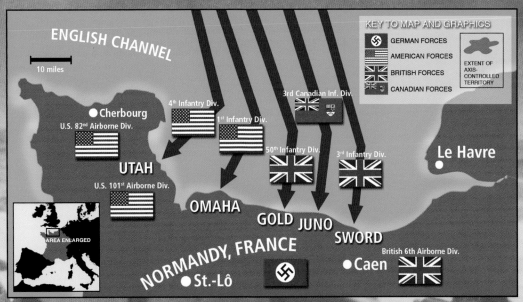

KEY TO MAP AND GRAPHICS

GERMAN FORCES
AMERICAN FORCES
BRITISH FORCES
CANADIAN FORCES

EXTENT OF AXIS-CONTROLLED TERRITORY

ENGLISH CHANNEL

10 miles

4th Infantry Div.

1st Infantry Div.

3rd Canadian Inf. Div.

Cherbourg

U.S. 82nd Airborne Div.

UTAH

U.S. 101st Airborne Div.

AREA ENLARGED

50th Infantry Div.

3rd Infantry Div.

Le Havre

OMAHA

GOLD   JUNO

SWORD

NORMANDY, FRANCE

St.-Lô

Caen

British 6th Airborne Div.

On June 6, 1944, American, British, and Canadian forces stormed the coast of Normandy, in northern France. The beaches were divided into five sections: Utah, Omaha, Gold, Juno, and Sword. American and British airborne troops also took part in the invasion against well-defended German forces.

JUNE 1944

Supreme Allied Commander U.S. Army General Dwight D. Eisenhower encourages paratroopers of the U.S. 101st Airborne Division—the "Screaming Eagles"—a day before the D-Day invasion. Paratroopers, many carried by silent glider aircraft, landed in France the night before the main invasion. They succeeded in securing critical bridges and roads despite heavy losses.

Stormy seas almost delayed the invasion, but Eisenhower took advantage of a break in the weather and designated June 6, 1944, as D-Day. In the early morning hours, a vast flotilla of more than 5,000 ships carrying 175,000 soldiers, 50,000 vehicles and other equipment crossed the English Channel toward the coast of Normandy, France. Overhead flew more than 11,000 fighters and bombers in support of the invasion.

The troops landed on five different beaches spread out over 50 miles (80 km) of coastline. The beaches were code named Utah, Omaha, Gold, Juno, and Sword. American forces landed on Utah and Omaha Beaches, while the

'*The Tanks Go In*', *Sword Beach*, a painting by Richard Willis depicting the British amphibious assault at Sword Beach on D-Day.

British took Gold and Sword Beaches. Canadian soldiers landed on Juno Beach.

Landing craft—called Higgins boats—took the troops close to the beaches, then dropped their front ramps. The troops rushed out, directly into enemy machine gun fire. Many were also killed when they accidentally landed in deep water and were unable to swim with their heavy packs.

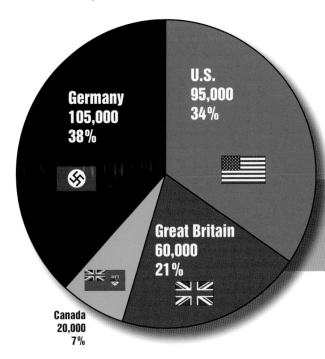

Germany
105,000
38%

U.S.
95,000
34%

Great Britain
60,000
21%

Canada
20,000
7%

The number of troops from major countries fighting in Normandy, France, on D-Day, June 6, 1944.

Above left: American soldiers take cover in a ditch near the town of Ste.-Sauveur-le-Vicomte during the Normandy invasion. *Above right:* An American soldier shares a laugh with a woman in the liberated town of Ste.-Mère-Église, France.

The German defenses at Normandy were under the command of Field Marshal Erwin Rommel. A series of mines, bunkers, artillery, and machine gun nests—called the Atlantic Wall by Adolf Hitler—meant tough going for Allied troops. Casualties were high on both sides.

Worst of all was Omaha Beach. The landing zone was heavily defended, with high bluffs. More than 5,000 young Americans were killed or wounded on this six-mile (10-km) strip of sand on D-Day.

Total Allied casualties were about 10,000 killed or wounded. But the mission was a daring success. Within days, enough men and equipment arrived to start moving inland. Paris was liberated by August 25. The American Third Army, commanded by General George Patton, pushed the enemy back toward Germany. The Nazis in Western Europe were finally on the run.

Allied ships unload troops plus a massive amount of equipment at Omaha Beach on June 7, 1944. The balloons in the sky above the beach keep low-flying enemy fighter planes from strafing troops on the ground.

GLOSSARY

ALLIES

The Allies were the many nations that were allied, or joined, in the fight against Germany, Italy, and Japan in World War II. The most powerful nations among the Allies included the United States, Great Britain, the Soviet Union, France, China, and Canada.

AXIS

The Axis powers were the World War II alliance of Germany, Italy, and Japan.

BLITZKRIEG

A German word meaning "lightning warfare." It described a new strategy that the German military used in World War II. *Blitzkrieg* called for very large invasions to overwhelm the enemy quickly with combined land and air attacks in order to avoid long, drawn-out battles.

CASUALTY

Soldiers and civilians reported as either killed, wounded, or missing in action.

D-DAY

A day when a military operation begins. Most people today associate D-Day with the Normandy invasion of June 6, 1944.

HIGGINS BOAT

A landing craft (boat) designed by American Andrew Higgins used in amphibious assaults. They were used to transport troops from larger ships up to the beaches during an attack. A Higgins boat could carry about 36 soldiers to shore. After a ramp was lowered onto the beach, the soldiers exited the boat through the bow. Higgins boats were very important in successful Allied amphibious assaults, like those at D-Day in Normandy, France, and in many islands of the Pacific Ocean. Supreme Allied Commander U.S. Army General Dwight Eisenhower once said, "Andrew Higgins is the man who won the war for us. If Higgins had not designed and built those [boats], we never could have landed over an open beach. The whole strategy of the war would have been different."

NAZI

The Nazi Party was the political party in Germany that supported Adolf Hitler. After 1934 it was the only political party allowed in Germany. This is when Hitler became a dictator and ruled Germany with total power.

A French tribute to a fallen American soldier in Normandy, France.

INDEX